Guide to the Masterpieces of the
Sistine Chapel

Presentation by *Antonio Paolucci*
Texts by *Paola Di Giammaria, Giovanna Uzzani*

EDIZIONI MUSEI VATICANI

GIUNTI  sillabe

ISBN 978-88-8271-249-5

© 2013 Edizioni Musei Vaticani
Città del Vaticano
www.museivaticani.va

Editorial Direction
Direzione dei Musei

Texts
Paola Di Giammaria (pp. 5-13; 107-111)
Giovanna Uzzani (pp. 15-19; 37-43)

Copyediting
Ufficio Pubblicazioni Musei Vaticani

Photographs
© Servizio Fotografico Musei Vaticani

Executive Editors
Giunti Editore S.p.A.
Via Bolognese 165 - 50139 Firenze - Italia
Via Borgogna 5 - 20122 Milano - Italia
www.giunti.it

s i l l a b e s.r.l.
Scali d'Azeglio 22 - 57123 Livorno - Italia
www.sillabe.it - info@sillabe.it

Editorial Direction
Claudio Pescio
Maddalena Paola Winspeare

Graphic Project
Studio Contri Toscano, Firenze

Translation
Russell Hall

Heartfelt thanks for their collaboration go to
Scala Group S.p.A.

First edition: June 2013

Printed by Tipografia Vaticana

Reprinted   Year

5 4 3 2 1 0   2015 2014 2013

Summary

My thoughts are directed towards the roughly twenty thousand people who each day enter the Sistine Chapel, fatal attraction, and unmissable objective for anyone who comes to Rome and visits the Museums of the Pope. There are people of every provenance, every language, every religion or, as is ever more frequent nowadays, of no religion. They are people who, in the vast majority of cases, have neither a historical-artistic or humanistic grounding. To this type of visitor, entering the Sistine Chapel provokes a sort of consternation. This is not a case of the so-called "Stendhal's Syndrome", cited too often in error. Rather it is confusion and bewilderment; a dizzying interpretative tumult. Who are they, what are the countless figures supposed to represent; that tangle of nudes, those ancient and solemn images? Many, especially the more elderly of Catholic extraction, will see floating in those frescoes, disjointed fragments of the Catechism of their infancy. Many will sense feelings gleaned from advertising images, absorbed from newspapers and the television. For example, in the "electric" scene which unites the finger of Adam with that of God the creator. For everyone will predominate the media clamour that, fed by mythography and legend, surrounds the name of Michelangelo. In effect, only a small minority among the multitude who enter the Sistine Chapel will know how to correctly decodify the subjects represented; know how to arrange them in historical-scriptural order; connect them to the appropriate Biblical text; appreciate the iconographic originality and artistic specificity. These will realise, and it is an emotional and all-absorbing feeling, that the Sistine Chapel in its entirety is not only one of the high points of human civilisation. It is much more. It is the *historia salutis*; the destiny of each and every one who finds comfort in images that have in the Scriptures, their justification and foundation. There is the alpha and the omega in the Sistine Chapel; there is the origin of the world and its ending; there are the Prophets and the Sibyls who announce, from the abyss of the centuries, the coming of the Saviour. There is Christ who brings His Law to complete and supersede that of Moses. All these things make up the system of primary meanings that innervate and sustain the pictorial cycles of the Sistine Chapel, rendering this place a true visual Catechism; the defining sanctuary of the Roman Catholic Church. It was opportune that someone connected to the Sistine Chapel in all its complexity, with its buildings and with its symbolic meanings, realised the need to speak not to the experts who for professional reasons already possess the appropriate knowledge, but to a cultivated public which desires to be informed in a mode which is simple, clear, and effective, yet nonetheless, scientifically impeccable. So here is the book that my lines introduce; the latest product of the Edizioni Musei Vaticani, realised by Giunti and Sillabe. It has been put together by Paola Di Giammaria and Giovanna Uzzani, two art historian colleagues, both well-known and esteemed by me. The former because she works in the Vatican Museums which I direct, with responsibilty for running the Photographic Library; the latter since she is a friend of long standing, and a former sound collaborator in the years in which I was Head of the Florentine Museums. To both I give my sincere gratitude for their excellent work, which has now been consigned to print.

Antonio Paolucci
Director of the Vatican Museums

From Cappella Magna to Sistine Chapel

On 29th September 1420, with the triumphal entry into Rome of Pope Martin V (Colonna, 1417-1431), a member of one of the most ancient families of the city, an end came to the Western Schism that for nearly forty years, from 1378 to 1417, had lacerated the Occidental Church in the wake of the conflict between Popes and antipopes for the control of the papal throne. The schism had followed on from the disastrous period of exile of the Popes in Avignon, which had resolved itself with the return of the Apostolic See to Rome at the behest of Gregory XI (de Beaufort, 1371-1378) in 1377, after about seven decades of sojourn in the French town. Riding in triumph from the Sant'Angelo Bridge towards the Vatican, flanked by the exultant masses, Martin V crossed a city that had been tested by centuries of neglect, by the ravages of civil war, and by the devastation of time. Following his election, the revival of Rome began slowly but surely, continuing under the pontificate of Nicholas V (Parentucelli, 1447-1455), a highly cultured personage, who loved to surround himself with scholars and artists. Beato Angelico (Brother Giovanni da Fiesole, known as Beato Angelico, c.1395-1455) was summoned in order to fresco the walls of the Niccolina Chapel, adjacent to the Pope's private quarters from which it takes its name, with *Scenes from the Lives of Saints Stephen and Laurence*.

Rome once more became the centre of cultural, political and religious life, thanks to a vast programme of urban reorganisation, and a renewal of ancient Christian monuments heavily promoted by the Pope. The Vatican Buildings and their environs could not fail to be part of this project.

The Pope initiated the expansion of the Apostolic Palace with the realisation of a building on three levels, paying particular attention to the high symbolic value of the so-called Cappella Magna, dating from the Mediaeval era, and which needs to be distinguished from the previously mentioned Niccolina Chapel; a "snug and secret" chapel in which the Pope celebrated mass on a daily basis. In essence, the Cappella Magna would have to be a space dedicated to the devotional and ceremonial needs of the Pope, as well as to the dispositions of the courtly calendar.

Nicholas V determined to elevate the ancient Chapel to the highest splendour, taking inspiration from the magnificence of the legendary Temple of Solomon, the first temple in Jerusalem, constructed in the X Century BC, and destroyed by the Babylonians in the VI Century BC.

The pontiff's resolutions were taken on by his successor, Sixtus IV (della Rovere, 1471-1484), a former professor of theology and Minister General of the Franciscans, who provided a great cultural boost to the politics of the entire pontifical court with the increase in artistic and decorative projects of ample breadth. To him is owed the flowering of antiquarian passion, culminating in the inauguration of the Vatican Library and the nomination in 1475 of the Humanist Bartolomeo Sacchi, known as Platina (1421-1481), as its first Prefect. An account of this can be seen in the fresco by

Melozzo da Forlì (1438-1494), which depicts the consignment of the Library keys to Platina on the part of Sixtus IV. This can be viewed today in the Vatican Pinacoteca. The Pope also invested in great building projects, including the creation of the Sixtus Bridge, inaugurated during the Jubilee of 1475, which served to facilitate access to St. Peter's for pilgrims arriving from the left bank of the Tiber, who had previously been obliged to cram together on the Sant'Angelo Bridge. However, his most important project – that which took his name and ensured it a place in history – was the completion of a new pontifical chapel on the site of the ancient Cappella Magna. Sixtus IV utilised the mediaeval chapel for the first six years of his pontificate, before deciding in 1477, as part of the renewal of the Vatican, to incorporate a part of the walls of the primitive edifice into the still extant Sistine Chapel, from whom it

External View of the
Sistine Chapel

Melozzo da Forlì
(1438-1494)
Sixtus IV and Platina,
1477 circa
Vatican Pinacoteca

inherited its name. Thus the Sistine rose from the remains of the
Cappella Magna, also taking inspiration from the grandiose chapel
set up in the Papal Palace in Avignon; this also being situated on
the top floor of the building. It was designed so as to incorporate
the foundations of the older building, which was rectangular in
form; 40 metres in length and roughly 13 in width. Nothing is
known regarding the height and covering of the Cappella Magna,
but it was located in the centre of the pontifical palace realised by
Nicholas III (Orsini, 1277-1280). Its plan displayed irregularities,
with the side walls converging towards the base wall, which, in

turn, is not perfectly parallel with that containing the entrance. Such anomalies, difficult to reconcile with the rational, humanistic mentality characteristic of the late 1400s, were analysed in the context of an intervention aimed at the global revival of a pre-existent structure which was to be overlayed by the new chapel. The construction materials of the older building were, in fact, incorporated up to the level of the window-sills, from which point the masonry of the Sistine Chapel itself commences.

The ceremonial importance of the liturgical functions that took place in the chapel called for an ambient capable of expressing the concept of papal majesty, not least on occasions linked to the diplomatic and political activities of the Holy See that were enacted here. The Pope had a private chapel destined for daily use - Sixtus IV made use of the Niccolina - nevertheless, the liturgical calendar envisaged functions and events that, at times, would be celebrated in the Basilica of St. Peter's, but more frequently in the large pontifical chapel situated in the palace. From its very beginnings, the vast space was divided by a monumental screen or *transenna*, intended to separate the true papal chapel from the area reserved for guests and political personages, who could thus assist at the ceremonies without, however, mingling with the pontifical court itself. It is the Florentine architect Baccio Pontelli (1450-1492) that the noted 16th Century biographer Giorgio Vasari (1511-1574) credits with the design of the Sistine Chapel; initiated in 1477 and completed in the summer of 1481, under the direction of the architect Giovannino de' Dolci. Several documents testify to the latter having been paid for work on the chapel. In February 1486,

Interior View of the
Sistine Chapel

The Vault

by which time Giovannino had died, his son Cristoforo was still receiving payment for the construction of the large chapel. The structure was thus terminated in a relatively brief time, especially taking into account the historical-political situation of the Papacy, which at that time was engaged in war against Florence, which only came to an end in December 1480.

The interior of the Sistine Chapel, the proportions of which are equal to those of the Temple of Solomon as it is described in the Old Testament, is covered by a flattened barrel vault, connected to the walls by spandrels and pendentives, and illuminated by six great windows that open out on both of the lateral walls. A further pair of windows, originally present in the wall behind the altar, were plastered over in order to enable Michelangelo (Michelangelo Buonarroti, 1475-1564) to realise the *Last Judgement*.

The Sistine Chapel is known all over the world as the place in which the pontiff is elected. Initially, along its walls, were predisposed the cells in which the cardinals were hosted for the entire period of voting. This practice was abandoned as the number of cardinals participating in the Conclave grew. The cardinals, gathered together in total isolation, make use of a stove equipped with a long tube, from which black or white smoke wafts out in order to communicate to the congregation in St. Peter's Square the result of every vote.

The Cosmati floor, detail

The Decoration of the Sistine Chapel: the Floor, the Transenna and the Chancel

The floor, made up of marble inlaying inspired by the great tradition of the Cosmati family, Roman masters of marble maquetry active in the XII and XIII Centuries, covers and delineates the ceremonial walkway that leads from the entrance to the altar; emphasing the position of the Papal Throne and the cardinals' seats, as well as the movements of the celebrants. In this manner the geometric patterns take on an extremely important role in the delineating of liturgical space, in that they confer order to the ceremonies and indicate a suitable disposition for the participants. Originally the transenna divided the chapel into two sections of equal size, and only subsequently was it placed in its current position, that is superimposed over the first of the decorative circles. Entering the chapel from the main door, six circles that form a continuous spiral in the direction of the altar can be observed. The circle nearest to the entrance was created using porphyry, a material much appreciated at the time of the Roman Empire for its bright pink colour, and associated with imperial pomp, given that it was only used for works of art destined for the emperor and the inner circle of his family. In imperial cerimonies it was the custom to kneel on *rotae* of porphyry to render homage to the emperor. These are, in effect, the so-called *rota porphyiretica*, which are visible in the same position in the principal Roman churches (including the

ancient and modern Basilicas of St. Peter), and indicate the point at which the celebrant or worshipper should stop to genuflect. Once past the transenna, geometric squares outline the seats of the cardinals, placed symmetrically on three sides, leaving open the fourth facing towards the altar. At the sides, between the squares and the three steps leading to the altar, were hosted in perpendicular rows, participants who were inferior in rank to the pontifical family. The Pope would sit on his throne to their left. The geometric forms in front of the altar indicated the positions to be used by the celebrant. The screen takes the form of a splendid marble transenna, which together with the chancel, forms part of the lapidary ornamentation envisaged by Sixtus IV for the Chapel, along with the pictorial decorations for the walls. The transenna makes clear reference to *iconostasis*, a low wall decorated with marble slabs, on which icons were hung. In Paleo-Christian churches these separated the presbytery from the zone reserved for the congregation. In the Sistine Chapel it carries out the same function, dividing the more spacious area destined for religious ceremonies from the smaller part in which laymen and women gather. The marble panels decorated with festoons of fruit and *putti* holding up the coat of arms of Sixtus IV, support a grille between small marble pillars and an architrave with eight candelabras (originally seven), which recall the

The Cosmati floor, detail

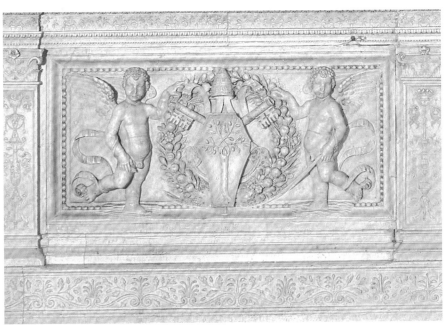

Mino da Fiesole
(1431-1484) and assistants
Marble Transenna and
details of a
panel, 1471-1484

candelabra with seven arms kept in the Temple in Jerusalem.
Equally splendid is the chancel in the right wall, this being the
area dedicated to the choir which accompanied the celebrations
with their singing. In fact, it was Sixtus IV himself, not long after
his election, who created the College of Chaplain Singers, the first
nucleus of the future Sistine Chapel Choir (Cappella Musicale
Pontificia "Sistina").
A long stone bench runs around the entire perimeter of the chapel,
with the exception of the area above the steps in the wall where the
altar is situated.

The Fifteenth Century Sistine Cycle

The Sistine Chapel has always been synonymous with Michelangelo, whose frescoes have to a certain extent altered the original decoration commissioned by Sixtus IV. The XV Century decoration nevertheless conditioned every subsequent intervention to the interior of the Chapel, including that undertaken by the great Tuscan master. On 15 August 1483, the Feast of the Assumption, the Pope inaugurated the Chapel with its recently completed frescoes. Thus Sixtus IV had brought the Renaissance to Rome.

The organisation of the frescoes seems to have been conceived in strict accordance with architectonic features, thereby leading to an indissoluble unity. Six panels follow one another on each of the principal walls, giving a total of twelve, rather than the sixteen originally envisaged. The decoration is laid out in three series above the four walls. The lower zone is decorated with false curtains, coloured yellow or blue, the heraldic colours of the family of Sixtus IV; these being divided by elegantly decorated pilaster strips. The intermediate register hosts the symmetrical unfolding of stories from the Old and New Testaments - the stories of Moses and Christ, on the left and right walls respectively - which depart from the altar walls before concluding on the walls near the entrance. In the upper strip are housed the portraits of twenty-eight pontiffs in false niches.

The sequence of pontiffs originally began on the altar wall; that on which Michelangelo would paint the *Last Judgement*. Christ and Peter were depicted, along with Linus and Anacletus, the next in the papal succession. At the centre of the wall there was formerly an altar-piece by Perugino (Pietro Vannucci, known as il Perugino, 1450-1523), depicting the *Assumption of the Virgin Mary*. In the upper zone, there were two scenes; the *Finding of Moses in the Waters* and the *Birth of Jesus*, subsequently destroyed to make way for Michelangelo's fresco.

The vaulted ceiling was painted in 1479-1480 by the Umbrian painter Piermatteo D'Amelia (1445/48-c.1506) in imitation of a sky, with golden stars on a background of blue lapis lazzuli.

The complex iconographic programme sought to affirm pontifical authority. Moses, the guide of the chosen people, prefigures Christ. Both are legislators; Moses that of the Old Testament, Jesus that of the New. The primary Law is fully realsed in the evangelical teachings of Christ. Thereafter it is realised in the second Law, whose power is transmitted through time to Peter and his successors. The enterprise was the fruition of a collaboration between a team of painters who pledged to follow a common approach, both from the point of view of content as well as with regards to choices of style and colour, under the direction of the decoration's commissioner and his court of theologists.

Sandro Botticelli (Alessandro Filipepi, 1445-1510), Domenico Ghirlandaio (1449-1494), Cosimo Rosselli (1439-1507) and Perugino were bound by the contract of 27 October 1481 to realise ten frescoes by the 15 March of the following year, with the help of their collaborators. It was agreed that decoration should begin *a capite altaris*, that is, above the altar. These four masters were all linked by their Florentine background, and in particular to the figure of Lorenzo de' Medici, known as the Magnificent (1449-1492), for whom they had previously worked. The first three were Florentine by birth; the fourth by adoption. In fact, upon arriving in Florence, the latter's career as a painter commenced in the workshop of Verrochio (Andrea di Michele Cioni, known as il Verrocchio, 1437-1488). The summoning of Lorenzo the Magnificent's artists to Rome was made possible, or at least rendered more favourable, also thanks to the historical-political situation of the era, during which a new climate of peace was established between Florence and the Popes. The last painter to join the group was Luca Signorelli (1445-1523), who realised on the left wall the scene depicting the *Testament of Moses* and on the entrance wall the *Dispute over the Body of Moses*.

On this latter wall two original paintings, the one by Signorelli and the *Resurrection of Christ* by Domenico Ghirlandaio, were lost in 1522 following structural subsidence, and were reproduced towards

View of the North Wall

the end of the XVI Century by Matteo da Lecce (1547-1616) and Hendrick van den Broeck (1519-1597); adherents of the final Mannerist school.

The Sistine painters were provided with common guidelines with regard to the general impostation of the decoration, so as to ensure that a certain degree of homogeneity be respected without each artist's individuality being compromised. The dimensions and the proportions of the figures would have to be uniform from the point of view of the observer. Decorative coherence was also rendered possible thanks to the adoption of a standard dimensional scale for the figures; to the use of a recurring rythmic lay-out and structure; and the utilisation of a set of dominant tonalities, among which the abundance of finishing touches in gold stand out. These serve to intensify the light with effects that would have appeared particularly suggestive in the glow of torches and candles. It is important to note that the stories of Christ and Moses reflect each other. The correspondences between each pair of scenes, the one in front of the other, are made explicit by the overlying inscriptions, which take on the role of didactic captions whose aim is to interpret the

View of the South Wall

tribulations of Moses as being the precursors of those of Christ. Thus, if on the left wall Perugino painted the *Journey of Moses in Egypt*, on the opposite wall the same painter depicted the *Baptism of Christ*. With these two scenes the Sistine cycle begins.

According to the most reliable sources, it was Perugino who was given the role of coordinating the squad of above-mentioned painters, along with a variety of assistants, among whom should be cited Piero di Cosimo (1461-1521), Biagio D'Antonio (1466-1515), and Bartolomeo della Gatta (1448-1502).

On the left wall the cycle continues with *Episodes from the Life of Moses* by Botticelli, who painted opposite it the *Temptations of Christ*, in which the central episode takes place in the background whilst in the foreground, in accordance with veterotestamentary tradition, a scene of sacrifice unfolds. To the painting the *Crossing*

View of the East Wall
(Entrance Wall)

of the Red Sea, the work of Biagio d'Antonio, is juxtaposed on the opposite wall the *Calling of the Apostles* by Ghirlandaio. This is followed by the *Handing Over of the Tablets of the Law*, in front of which is the *Sermon on the Mount*, a work by Cosimo Rosselli; and by Botticelli's scene depicting the *Punishment of Korah, Datan and Abiram*, which is mirrored by the *Handing Over of the Keys*, the most famous of the entire cycle, painted by Perugino. These final two paintings explicate the central message of the iconographic programme; that is, the affirmation of the divine origins of papal authority.

Perugino was entrusted with the most important fresco in doctrinal terms, the *Handing Over of the Keys*, in which is celebrated the transmission of Christ's powers to the first pontiff and thereby the institution of the papacy. The supremacy of Peter and subsequently of the Roman pontiffs thus becomes the rock upon which the universal Church is founded and sustained. In an idealised *piazza* converging on a central temple, to the sides of which two triumphal arches arise, Jesus hands Peter the keys to the Kingdom of Heaven; a symbol of the conferring of His power to the first earthly Vicar of Christ. The scene is extremely suggestive, and set out by the Umbrian master in a perfectly symmetrical manner: the lucid geometrical scansion of the floor serves to emphasise the way in which vanishing points converge on the temple, an octagonal, domed construction. The artist demonstrates that he has, in his use of space, made use of the notion of mathematical perspective derived from Piero della Francesca (c.1416/17-1492), another of the painting's points of reference.

Counterpointing the measured compositional order of the Umbrian painter is the restless fantasy of Botticelli, whose scene opposite, with its allusion to those who rebelled against Moses and suffered punishment, aims at restating the legitimacy of the supremacy of the Roman Church which, in accordance with its divine mandate, carries out its mission by defeating evil at all times. This is followed by the *Last Days of Moses*, a work by Luca Signorelli and Bartolomeo della Gatta, which faces the *Last Supper;* a fresco by Cosimo Rosselli and Biagio d'Antonio, set in an octagonal hall with a beautiful coffered ceiling.

The original cycle underlines the solemn political and doctrinal affirmation of the divine nature of the Pope and the intangibility of the powers conferred upon him. There is no doubt that the formulation of such a programmatic intervention took place under the direct guidance of Sixtus IV and his theologians. To achieve his aims he availed himself of the greatest painters of the era from the Umbro-Tuscan area, enlisting them travel to Rome along with their workshops. Requested of them was the capacity to interpret extremely complex subject matter with the height of style and a clarity of expression. The Sistine painters, in the brief time in which they realised the decoration (between the autumn of 1481 and the summer of 1483), opened the doors of the Vatican to the art of the Renaissance, to naturalism, to perspective, to compositional skill and a masterly use of colour.

The Chapel was later enriched with tapestries donated by Leo X (de' Medici, 1513-1521), today housed in the Vatican Pinacoteca, for which Raphael (Raffaello Sanzio, 1483-1520) designed the cartoons, subsequently finely woven in Brussels.

PERUGINO

The Journey of Moses in Egypt

Exodus 4, 18-20; 24-26:
Moses went back to his father-in-law Jethro and said to him, "Give me leave to return to my kinsmen in Egypt and see if they are still alive". And Jethro said to Moses, "Go in peace". Yahweh said to Moses in Midian, "Go, return to Egypt, for all those who wanted to kill you are dead". So Moses took his wife and his son and, putting them on a donkey, started back for Egypt; and Moses took the staff of God in his hand. ... On the journey, when he had halted for the night, Yahweh encountered him and tried to kill him. Then Zipporah, taking up a flint, cut off her son's foreskin and with it touched his feet and said, "You are my blood-bridegroom!". So he let him go. She said, "Blood-bridegroom" then, with reference to the circumcision.

SANDRO BOTTICELLI

Seven Episodes in the Life of Moses

Exodus 2, 11-21:
It happened one day, when Moses was grown up, that he went to see his kinsmen. While he was watching their forced labour he also saw an Egyptian striking a Hebrew, one of his kinsmen. Looking this way and that and seeing nobody in sight, he killed the Egyptian and hid him in the sand. On the following day he came back, and there were two Hebrews fighting. He said to the man who was in the wrong, "What do you mean by hitting your kinsman? And who appointed you," the man retorted, "to be prince over us and judge? Do you intend to kill me as you killed the Egyptian?". Moses was frightened. "Clearly that business has come to light," he thought. When Pharaoh heard of the matter, he tried to put Moses to death, but Moses fled from Pharaoh. He went into Midianite territory and sat down beside a well. Now there was a priest of Midian with seven daughters. They used to come to draw water and fill the troughs to water their father's flock. Some shepherds came and drove them away, but Moses sprang to their help and watered their flock. When they returned to their father Reuel, he said to them "Why are you back so early today?". "An Egyptian protected us from the shepherds," they said, "And he even drew water for us and watered the flock". "And where is he", he asked his daughters. "Why did you leave the man there? Ask him to eat with us". Moses agreed to stay on there with the man, who gave him his daughter Zipporah in marriage.
Exodus 3, 1-5:
Moses was looking after the flock of his father-in-law, Jethro, the priest of Midian; he led it to the farside of the desert and came to Horeb, the mountain of God.

The angel of Yahweh appeared to him in a flame blazing from the middle of a bush. Moses looked; there was the bush blazing, but the bush was not being burnt up ... God called to him from the middle of the bush and said. "Come no nearer! Take off your sandals, for the place where you are standing is holy ground!".
Exodus 13, 17-18:
When Pharaoh had let the people go, ... God did not let them take the road to the Philistines' territory.

BIAGIO D'ANTONIO
Passing of the Red Sea

Exodus 14, 15-31; 15,1:
Yehweh then said to Moses, "Why cry out to me? Tell the Israelites to march on. Your part is to raise your staff and stretch out your hand over the sea and divide it, so that the Israelites can walk through the sea on dry ground … ".
The Egyptians gave chase, and all Pharaoh's horses, chariots and horsemen went into the sea after them … Moses stretched out his hand over the sea and, as day broke, the sea returned to its bed … The returning waters washed right over the chariots and horsemen of Pharaoh's entire army, which had followed the Israelites into the sea; not a single one of them was left. …
It was then that Moses and the Israelites sang this song in Yahweh's honor.

COSIMO ROSSELLI

The Handing Over of the
Tables of the Law

Exodus 19, 1-3:
Three months to the day after leaving Egypt, the Israelites reached the desert of Sinai.
Setting out from Rephidim, they reached the desert of Sinai and pitched camp in the desert; there, facing the mountain, Israel pitched camp.
Moses then went up to God, and Yahweh called to him from the mountain, saying, "Say this to the House of Jacob! Tell the Israelites". ...

Exodus 24, 12:
Yahweh said to Moses, "Come up to me on the mountain. Stay there, and I will give you the stone tablets, the law and the commandment which I have written for their instruction".
Exodus 32, 1-20:
When the people saw that Moses was a long time before coming down the mountain, they gathered round Aaron and said to him, "Get to work, make us a god to go at our head; for that Moses, the man who brought us here from Egypt, we do not know what has become of him". Aaron replied, "Strip off the gold rings in the ears of your wives and your

sons and daughters, and bring them to me". The people all stripped off the gold rings from their ears and brought them to Aaron. He received what they gave him, melted it down in a mould and with it made the statue of a calf. "Israel," the people shouted, "here is your God who brought you here from Egypt!". Observing this, Aaron built an altar before the statue and made this proclamation, "Tomorrow will be a feast in Yahweh's honour". ... Yahweh then said to Moses, "Go down at once, for your people whom you brought here from Egypt have become corrupt". They have quickly left the way which I ordered them to follow. They have cast themselves a metal calf, worshipped it and offered sacrifice to it, shouting, "Israel, here is your God who brought you here from Egypt!". ... Moses turned and came down the mountain with the two tablets of the Testimony in his hands, tablets inscribed on both sides, inscribed on the front and on the back. ... And there, as he approached the camp, he saw the calf and the groups dancing. Moses blazed with anger. He threw down the tablets he was holding, shattering them at the foot of the mountain. He seized the calf they had made and burned it, grinding it into powder which he scattered on the water, and made the Israelites drink it.

SANDRO BOTTICELLI
Punishment of Korah, Datan and Abiram

Numbers 16, 1-35:
Now Korah … and Datan and Abiram … rebelled against Moses … Moses said to Korah "You and all your party, come before Yahweh tomorrow, you and they and Aaron too. Each will take his censer, put incense in it, and bring his censer before Yahweh - two hundred and fifty censers …".
The moment he finished saying all this, the ground split apart under their feet, the earth opened its mouth and swallowed them, their families, all Korah's people and all their property … Fire then shot out from Yahweh and consumed the two hundred and fifty men offering incense.

LUCA SIGNORELLI
The Last Days of Moses

Deuteronomy 5, 1:
Moses called all Israel together and said to them, "Listen, Israel, to the laws and customs that I proclaim to you today. Learn them and take care to observe them".
Deuteronomy 31, 1-7:
Moses went and spoke to all Israel as follows: … "Joshua too will lead you across, as Yahweh has said". Moses then summoned Joshua and, in the presence of all Israel, said to him, "Be strong, stand firm; you will be the one to go with this people into

the country which Yahweh has sworn to their ancestors that he would give them; you are to be the one who puts them into possession of it".
Deuteronomy 34, 1-7:
Then, leaving the Plains of Moab, Moses went up Mount Nebo, the peak of Pisgah opposite Jericho. Yahweh showed him the whole country. … Yahweh said to him, "This is the country which I promised on oath to give to Abraham, Isaac and Jacob, saying: I shall give it to your descendants. I have allowed you to see it for yourself, but you will not cross into it". There in the country of Moab, Moses, servant of Yahweh, died as Yahweh decreed. … Moses was a hundred and twenty years old when he died.

PERUGINO

The Baptism of Christ

Matthew 3, 13-15:
Then Jesus appeared: he came from Galilee to
the Jordan to be baptised by John. John tried to
dissuade him, with the words, "It is I who need
baptism from you, and yet you come to me!".
But Jesus replied, "Leave it like this for the time
being; it is fitting that we should, in this way, do
all that uprightness demands". Then John gave in
to him.

SANDRO BOTTICELLI
The Temptations of Christ

Mark 1, 12-13:
And at once the Spirit drove him into the desert
and he remained there for forty days, and was
put to the test by Satan. He was with the wild
animals, and the angels looked after him.

DOMENICO GHIRLANDAIO

Vocation of the First Apostles

Matthew 4, 18-19:

As he was walking by the sea of Galilee he saw two brothers, Simon, who is called Peter and his brother Andrew, casting a net into the sea (for they were fishermen). And he said to them "Come, follow me, and I will make you fishers of men".

COSIMO ROSSELLI

The Sermon on the Mount

Matthew 5, 3-7:

How blessed are the poor in spirit: the kingdom of Heaven is theirs. Blessed are the gentle: they shall have the earth as inheritance. Blessed are those who mourn: they shall be comforted. Blessed are those who hunger and thirst for uprightness: they shall have their fill. Blessed are the merciful: they shall have mercy shown them.

PERUGINO
Handing Over of the Keys

Matthew 16, 18-19:
" ... And I say to thee, thou art Peter, and upon this rock I will build my Church, and the gates of hell shall not prevail against it. And I will give thee the keys of the kingdom of heaven; and whatever thou shall bind on earth shall be bound in heaven, and whatever thou shalt loose on earth shall be loosed in heaven".

COSIMO ROSSELLI

Last Supper

Matthew 26, 26:
And while they were at supper, Jesus took bread,
and blessed and broke, and gave it to his disciples,
and said "Take and eat, this is my body".

ERITHRAEA

The Vault of the Chapel:
The Frescoes of Michelangelo
(1508-1512)

In the spring of 1504, due to problems of static balance caused by its irregular foundations, a large crack appeared in the vault of the Chapel and the star-spangled sky originally painted by Piermatteo d'Amelia was damaged by the subsidence. Already at this time, in the mind of Julius II (della Rovere, 1503-1513), nephew of Sixtus IV, began to form the idea of commissioning Michelangelo to replace the decoration. The Tuscan master had first been summoned to Rome by Julius II in 1505 in the role of sculptor, with the task of designing the pontiff's tomb, which would be placed within the Basilica of St. Peter, then undergoing construction. However, fierce disagreement sprang up between the two of them. While the sculptor went ahead elaborating a grandiose and extremely expensive project, the Pope reserved his attention and his funds for warfare and the titanic enterprise of reconstructing the Vatican Basilica. The assignment in the Sistine Chapel was greeted with stupour, and not a little downheartedness on the part of the artist, who considered himself to be a sculptor rather than a painter, and he was most reluctant to have put aside the ambitious project of the tomb of Julius II. Today this can be seen in its final version, much-reduced with respect to that originally conceived by the master, in the church of San Pietro in Vincoli in Rome.

The notion of a new decoration of the vault had certainly taken form in the spring of 1506, when Michelangelo received a letter from his friend Piero Rosselli, informing the former of the Pope's intention to assign the project to him, and of attempts at dissuasion on the part of Bramante (Donato Bramante, 1444-1514), architect of the Basilica of St Peter, who criticised Buonarroti for having little expertise in monumental painting. Under Julius II the Sistine Chapel had taken on a role of great importance in pontifical liturgical life, and it was inconceivable that it should be closed for years for the duration of the work. It therefore became necessary to erect a structure that would not impede with the celebration of sacred functions. The platform hanging from the roof, conceived by Bramante, was not to Michelangelo's liking, who projected another which was much more stable, given that it rested upon several beams protruding from the walls of the Chapel. Furthermore, its having steps also made it possible to fresco the spandrels and lateral lunettes in greater comfort. The official assignment is dated 10 May. The construction of the platform, the removal of the earlier decoration, and the rendering of the *arriccio* (that is, the preparatory layer of plaster) went on till the end of the July of that year. By the end of August 1510 the first half of the vault, from the Prophet *Zacharias* to the *Creation of Eve*, had been finished, but Julius II departed for Bologna, forcing the master to interrupt his work for a whole year. The brief amount of time that had lapsed between the assignment and the executive phase of such a complex enterprise reveals how the Pope and Michelangelo had already agreed upon the iconographic programme and decorative solution, which turned out to be much more ambitious than the initial project to represent the twelve Apostles on the vault in an antiquated manner.

On 14 and 15 August 1511 the pontiff paid a visit in order to inspect the part of the vault that had already been painted, and thus inaugurated the second phase of work. On 30 October 1512 the platform was dismantled once and for all, and the splendour of the vault was revealed to the eyes of all, *in primis* those of the Pope.

In the structure painted by the artist, the central strip is delineated by a fake marble frame and embellished by nine paintings of two differing sizes, which depict nine *Stories from Genesis*; the larger are found in proximity of the spandrels, the smaller above the thrones of the *Soothsayers* (that is, the *Prophets* and *Sibyls*) and are flanked by great fake bronze medallions, supported by ten pairs of *Ignudi* (nudes) sitting on stone plinths.

Proceeding from the entrance wall towards the altar wall we can observe the *Drunkenness of Noah*, the *Flood*, the *Sacrifice of Noah*, the *Original Sin*, the *Expulsion from Earthly Paradise*, the *Creation of Eve*, the *Creation of Man* (more commonly known as *of Adam*), the *Separation of the Land from the Waters*, the *Creation of the Sun, the Moon and the Plants*, and the *Separation of Light from Darkness*.

Below the marble frame that delineates the *Stories from Genesis*, twelve monumental thrones host the figures of the *Soothsayers*, five *Sibyls* and seven *Prophets*, who announce the birth of the Son of God. These substituted the twelve Apostles of the original project and are identifiable thanks to their underlying inscriptions. Eight spandrels appear in the intervals between the thrones, these being surmounted by a similar number of paired, bronzed nudes, which depict, along with the underlying lunettes, the *Ancestors of Christ*, from Abraham to Joseph, and form the strongest iconographical link between the biblical theme of the vault and the wall frescoes, dedicated to episodes from the New Testament. The four pendentives of the vault host four biblical stories that illustrate God's miraculous intervention in favour of His chosen people. Those to the sides of the entrance walls, *Judith and Holofernes* and *David and Goliath*; those flanking the altar walls, the *Punishment of Haman* and the *Brazen Serpent*.

The decoration of the vault thus served to complete the theological significance of the Sistine cycle on the walls. On the latter the parallel stories of Moses and Christ are unfurled – the former being emblematic of the Old Testament and a prefiguration of the new Law donated by God to humanity through the death and resurrection of the Son. On the vault was illustrated the history of mankind prior to receiving God's Law; from the creation of the world to the birth of Christ, announced by the Soothsayers.

Despite Bramante's attempt to convince the Pope not to assign the project to Michelangelo, concealing a feeling of envy with regard to the master as well an interest in having the work commissioned to his protégé, the young Raphael, it is certain that Michelangelo himself was not ignorant of the difficulties of the enterprise that lay ahead – for him new – to fresco an ample surface, over 20 metres high. In a sonnet addressed to a friend, he wrote: "Defend my dead painting from now on, Giovanni, and my honour, for I am not well placed, nor indeed a painter".

From the workshop of Ghirlandaio, where as a youth he had completed his apprenticeship, he summoned the assistants who would collaborate with him on the initial phases of the work,

Piermatteo d'Amelia
(1445/48-c.1506)
*Project for the XV Century
Decoration of the Vault
of the Sistine Chapel*,
1479-1480
Collection of Prints and
Drawings
of the Uffizi Gallery,
Florence

the names of whom have been handed down to us by Vasari. Francesco Granacci (c.1469-1543), with whom he had shared his youthful experience in the Medicean garden of San Marco in the happy season of Lorenzo the Magnificent, came to Rome, along with Giuliano Bugiardini (1475-1554), Jacopo di Sandro (dates unknown; active 1500-1554), who abandoned the platform in January 1508, and Jacopo di Lazzaro Torni, known as the *Indaco Vecchio* (*Old Indigo*) (1476-1526), who subsequently took his place. Of a different provenance, but still Florentine, were Angelo di Domenico di Donnino (1466-1513) and Bastiano da Sangallo (1481-1551), nephew of the more famous Giuliano, a friend and patron of Buonarroti. Granacci – who had links to Michelangelo going back to his childhood and who introduced the latter to Ghirlandaio's workshop – took on the role of right-hand man, both with regards to coordinating the various assistants, as well as carrying out tasks of a purely administrative nature.

While Ascanio Condivi, a biographer and contemporary of Michelangelo's, with the latter's authorisation expressly states that Michelangelo "finished the whole work in twenty months, without any help, not even an assistant to grind the colours"; Vasari, after having recalled the names of the Florentine painters, writes: "having begun the work, he got them to commence on several things as samples. However, regarding their efforts as in no way satisfying his desires, one morning he resolved to throw to the ground everything they had done. Thereafter he locked himself in the Chapel, not wanting to allow them in again". The two biographers, stretching the truth a bit, wanted to register the anomaly of the event with respect to the centuries-old tradition of the workshop. This version of the facts did, in effect, serve to spread the image of a temperamental and heroic Michelangelo, able to affront alone, years and years of years of backbreaking work, even putting his own health at risk.

The assistants did not enjoy the conditions of partial autonomy that were typical in other workshops, for example in that of Raphael, but instead were obliged to do work based on the master's cartoons, under the latter's strict control. As the most recent restoration has demonstated, the helpers (with the exception of Jacopo di Sandro) worked alongside the master until the end of 1509; that is, until the moment came to paint the final two scenes using the first platform, the *Original Sin* and the *Creation of Eve*.

In these two stories a radical change in the manner of representation can be discerned. The number of personages depicted diminishes, and as a consequence the proportions of the figures increases so as to reach a height of two metres. The aesthetic quality is great in every particular, with none of the lapses in quality that can be seen in the three scenes painted initially. Thus, in all probability, at this point Michelangelo decided to limit interventions on the part of his assistants, assigning them the execution of decorative tasks, such as the cornice and other secondary work. Granacci and Bugiardini returned to Florence, being replaced by less talented helpers, who were thus more suitable to undertake the menial tasks required by the master. From halfway along the surface of the vault, the hand of Michelangelo becomes exclusive. In any case, right from the start, he was uniquely responsible for the decoration; both in its inception and realisation. Michelangelo began to paint from the entrance wall of the Chapel, starting from the final part of the narrative.

View of the Vault

Having worked out the decorative scheme, he made sketches of the figures on a small scale. Subsequently he went on to a study of a life model of the whole figure, in magnificent pencil drawings in which anatomical precision is fused with an intense and refined rendering in chiaroscuro. The final phase envisaged the transposition of the drawings on to cartoons, carried out by the artist himself, and ultimately the transfer of the images to the wet plaster, via the technique of pouncing, constant in the first half of the vault, or direct incision, which is instead prevalent in the second half. It is probable that Michelangelo never realised a comprehensive drawing of the vault, but rather worked section by section. This becomes evident from the stylistic caesura between the two parts of the vault corresponding to the point where the work was interrupted for almost a year, following the unveiling of the first portion, which arrived at the *Creation of Eve*, the Prophet *Ezekiel* and the *Cuman Sibyl*. To this prime phase belong scenes of a more narrative nature, with the presence of numerous figures which act within landscapes. The narrative is introduced by the vigorous figures of the Prophets and Sibyls, the latter depicted as hieratic and puissant, distinct from earthly reality and absorbed in meditation. In the central portion Michelangelo wished to depict nine stories from the Book of Genesis in reverse chronological order; from the stories of Noah, the first in the the Hebrew line, backwards to scenes depicting the Creation. The first three sections to be realised were, in fact, those on the side by the entrance (the *Drunkenness of Noah*, the *Flood* and the *Sacrifice of Noah*), which present the protagonist Noah as the man saved from the flood and chosen by God following sin. Immediately after the scene illustrating the *Original Sin* is the *Expulsion from Earthly Paradise;* the first of three successive paintings dedicated to events linked to our Progenitors. The *Creation of Eve* is placed at the centre of the vault, in correspondence with the transenna that initially divided the Chapel in two equal parts, and thus, significantly, above the entrance to the area of the altar. On either side of this scene are the Prophet *Ezekiel,* who in his prophecies preannounced the birth of the Virgin Mary, and the *Cuman Sibyl,* of whom Virgil, in one of his *Eclogues* records the prophecy of the arrival of a boy born of a virgin, and destined to change the world.

The stories from Genesis also continue in the spandrels and lunettes, where the *Ancestors of Christ* are depicted, beginning with Noah's three sons. It is, in effect, a gallery with a wide variety of personages, some of whom are rapt in private contemplation. The colours become more candid and the technique is freer and more immediate. Between one scene and the next, the *Ignudi* (*Nudes*) serve to divulge the masterly attention which Michelangelo lavished on anatomical description and the positions of the bodies, thereby prefiguring later Mannerist solutions.

With the resumption of work in September 1511, as he gradually approached the altar walls, Michelangelo reduced the number of protagonists in the main scenes and eliminated environmental notations, leaving the figures the task of organising the space. These are depicted greatly foreshortened, with highly dynamic poses, which are decisively twisting so as to multiply the spatial directrixes. This is evident both in the central panels (the *Creation of Adam*), as well as in the final three scenes depicting the creation of the world (the *Separation of the Land from the Waters*, the *Creation of the Sun, the Moon and the Plants*, and the *Separation of Light from Darkness*), and finally in the scenes of the pendentives. The *Soothsayers* – larger than those which preceded them – burst into the space, barely containing themselves. Some seem to be possessed by a demon which agitates them (the *Libyan Sibyl*, the Prophet *Jonah*). The dynamism also invades the *Ignudi* in this portion of the vault, in which Michelangelo works through all the expressive potential of body movement, exceeding the 'Apollonian' limits which had guided the artist when depicting their companions.

The visual fulcrum of the narration is the scene depicting the *Creation of Adam*, recognised worldwide; the very symbol of the classical perfection inherent in Renaissance culture, a man created in the image of God. The gigantic body of the first man, in languid abandon, seems to shake itself and gain consciousness in front of our eyes, thanks to the divine spirit, which is the origin of every form of life. The extraordinary invention of the outstretched index fingers, caught an instant prior to the first contact, is a metaphor for the vital energy that flows from the Creator, whose figure is animated by a vigorous and inexorable force, to His creation.

In the course of the centuries following 31 October 1512, when the frescoes were unveiled to the Pope and the entire world, the cycle has undergone various cleanings, including the restorations carried out during the XVIII and XIX Centuries with the aim of revitalising its colours, and hiding the white salt stains which had been deposited on the frescoes due to the infiltration of rainwater. The restoration of the XV Century parietal decoration that took place in the 1960s, was followed by the great restoration that the Sistine Chapel underwent between 1979 and 1999 under the direction of Fabrizio Mancinelli, and carried out by Gianluigi Colalucci. This intervention, which unleashed a heated debate among experts and also roused public opinion, first involved the vault (1980-1989), and subsequently the *Last Judgement* (1990-1994). Immediately afterwards, from 1995 to 1999, the XV Century frescoes were restored, leading to a final result of great homogeneity.

The frescoes of the vault had finally been liberated from the blackening that had built up over the centuries, compromising their visibility; thereby allowing the colours to return to their original splendour, and ensuring that Michelangelo's inventions could be enjoyed anew.

Analyses carried out on these occasions demonstrated how Michelangelo possessed extraordinary dexterity and a complete mastery of the fresco technique, which enabled his painting to challenge dampness and survive for nearly five hundred years. He succeeded in combining the ancient techniques of the Florentine fresco tradition with shadows and finishing touches, added with vigour once the plaster had dried. This restoration, above all, has made it possible to evaluate the grandiose inheritance that Michelangelo left to the young adherents of Mannerism, both in terms of restlessness and dynamism, as well as in the revolutionary harmony of colours, the candid tones and the vibrant contrasts.

The season of the Renaissance was about to close, signalled definitively by the death of Raphael in 1520, giving way to a new and feverish research that would take place in the name of an a restless and tormented modernity.

Separation of Light from Darkness

Genesis 1, 1-4:
In the beginning God created heaven, and earth.
And the earth was void and empty, and darkness
was upon the face of the deep; and the Spirit of

God moved over the waters.
And God said: "Be light made!".
And light was made.
And God saw the light that it was good: and
God divided the light from the darkness.

Creation of Stars and Plants

Genesis 1, 14-15:
And God said: "Let there be lights made in the fermament of heaven, to divide the day and the night, and let them be for signs, and for seasons, and for days and years, 15 to shine in the firmament of heaven, and to give light upon the earth". And it was so done.

Separation of the Land from the Waters

Genesis 1, 9-10:
God also said: "Let the waters that are under the heaven be gathered together in one place; and let the dry land appear". And it was so done. And God called the dry land Earth; and the gathering together of the waters, he called Seas.

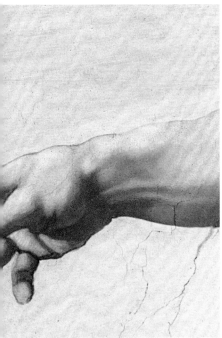

Creation of Adam

Genesis 2, 7:
… And the Lord God formed man of the slime
of the earth and breathed into his face the breath
of life, and man became a living soul.

Creation of Eve

Genesis 2, 21-22:
Then the Lord God cast a deep sleep upon Adam: and when he was fast asleep, he took one of his ribs, and filled up flesh for it. And the Lord God built the rib which he took from Adam into a woman: and brought her to Adam.

Original Sin

Genesis 3, 6-7; 17:
And the woman saw that the tree was good to
eat, and fair to the eyes, and delightful to behold:
and she took of the fruit thereof, and did eat.
And the eyes of them both were opened: and
when they perceived themselves to be naked …
And to Adam he said: "Because thou hast
hearkened to the voice of thy wife, and hast eaten
of the tree, whereof I commanded thee that thou
shouldst not eat, cursed is the earth in thy work;
with labour and toil shalt thou eat thereof all the
days of thy life".

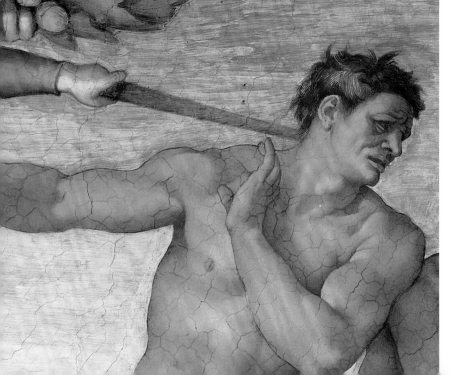

Sacrifice of Noah

Genesis 8, 20-21:
And Noah built an altar unto the Lord: and taking of all cattle and fowls that were clean, offered holocausts upon the altar. And the Lord smelled a sweet savour, and said: "I will no more curse the earth for the sake of man: for imagination and thought of man's heart are prone to evil from his youth; therefore I will no more destroy every living soul as I have done".

The Flood

Genesis 7, 15-17:
They went in to Noah into the ark, two and two
of all flesh, wherein was the breath of life.
And they that went in, went in male and female
of all flesh, as God had commanded him: and
the Lord shut him on the outside.
And the floor was forty days upon the earth, and
the waters increased, and lifted up the ark on
high from the earth.

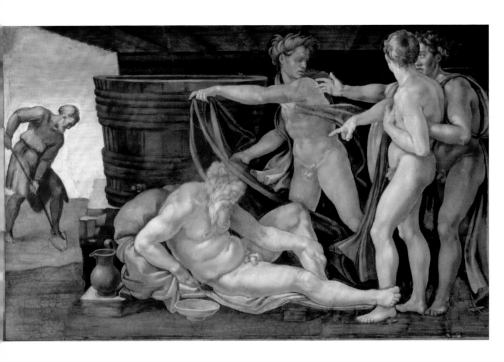

Drunkenness of Noah

Genesis 9, 20-23:
And Noah, a husbandman, began to till the ground, and planted a vineyard, and drinking of the wine was made drunk, and was uncovered in his tent. Which when Cham the father of Chanaan had seen, to wit, that his father's nakedness was uncovered, he told it to his two brethren outside. And Shem and Japheth took a robe, and putting it on their backs went in with their faces turned away, and put it over their father so that they might not see him unclothed.

Judith and Holofernes

Judith 13, 8-9:
And she struck twice upon his neck, and cut off
his head, and took off his canopy from the
pillars, and rolled away his headless body. And
after a while she went out, and delivered his head
of Holofernes to her maid.

David and Goliath

1 Samuel 17, 50-51:
Thus David triumphed over the Philistine with a
sling and a stone; he hit the Philistine and killed
him, though he had no sword in his hand. David
… seized his sword, pulled it from the scabbard,
despatched him and cut off his head.

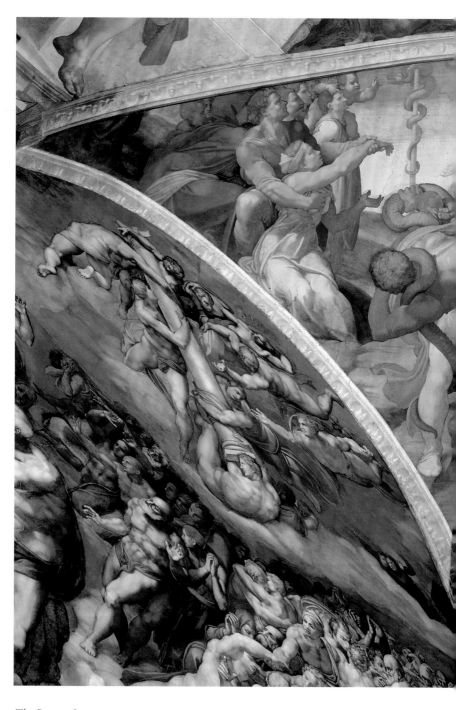

The Brazen Serpent

Numbers 21, 8:
And the Lord said to him "Make a brazen
serpent, and set it up for a sign; whosoever being
struck shall look on it, shall live".

Punishment of Aman

Esther 7, 9-10:
In the royal presence, Harbona, one of the officers, said, "There is that fifty-cubit gallows, too, which Haman ran up for Mordecai, who spoke up to the king's great advantage". It is all ready at his house. "Hang him on it", said the king. So Haman was hanged on the gallows which he had erected for Mordecai, and the king's wrath subsided.

Joab kills Abner

Bigdar threw the corpse of King Joram down from the chariot

2 Samuel 3, 27:
And when Abner reached Hebron Joab took him aside to the middle of the gate to speak to him treacheriously: and he stabbed him there in the groin, and he died, in revenge of the blood of Asael his brother.

2 Kings 9, 24-25:
But Jehu had drawn his bow; he struck Jehoram between the shoulder-blades, the arrow went through the king's heart, and he sank down in his chariot. "Pick him up", Jehu said to Bidkar, his equerry, "and throw him into the field … ".

Death of Urias

2 Samuel 11, 16-17:
Wherefore as Joab was besieging the city, he put Urias in the place where he knew the bravest men were.

And the men coming out of the city, fought against Joab and there fell some of the people of the servants of David, and Urias the Hethite was killed also.

*Jehu destroys
the worshippers of Baal*

2 Kings 10, 27:
And they brake down the image of Baal, and brake down the house of Baal, and made it a draught house unto this day.

*David kneeling in front of the Prophet
Nathan*

2 Samuel 12, 9:
Why therefore has thou despised the word of the Lord, to the evil in my sight? Thou hast killed Urias the Hethite with the sword and hast taken his wife to be thy wife, and hast slane him with the sword of the children of Ammon.

*Destruction of the
Achab Tribe*

2 Kings 10, 16-17:
So he made him ride in his chariot, and brought
him into Samaria. And he slew all that were left
of Achab in Samaria to a man, according to the
word of the Lord, which he spoke by Elias.

Death of Absalom

2 Samuel 18, 19:
And it happened that Absalom met the servants of David riding on a mule; and as the mule went under a thick and large oak his head stuck in the oak: and while he hung between the heaven and the earth, the mule on which he rode passed on.

Elijah on a Chariot of Fire

2 Kings 2, 11:
Now as they walked on, talking as they went, a chariot of fire appeared and horses of fire coming between the two of them, and Elijah went up to heaven in the whirlwind.

Abraham's Sacrifice

Genesis 22, 9-11:
And they came to the place which God had shown him, where he built an altar and laid the wood in order upon it; and when he had bound Isaac his son, he laid him on the altar upon the pile of wood. And he put forth his hand and took the sword to sacrifice his son. And behold the angel of the Lord called him from heaven.

Ignudi above the Prophet Joel

Ignudo above the Delphic Sibyl

Ignudi above the Eritrean Sibyl

Ignudi above the Prophet Isaiah

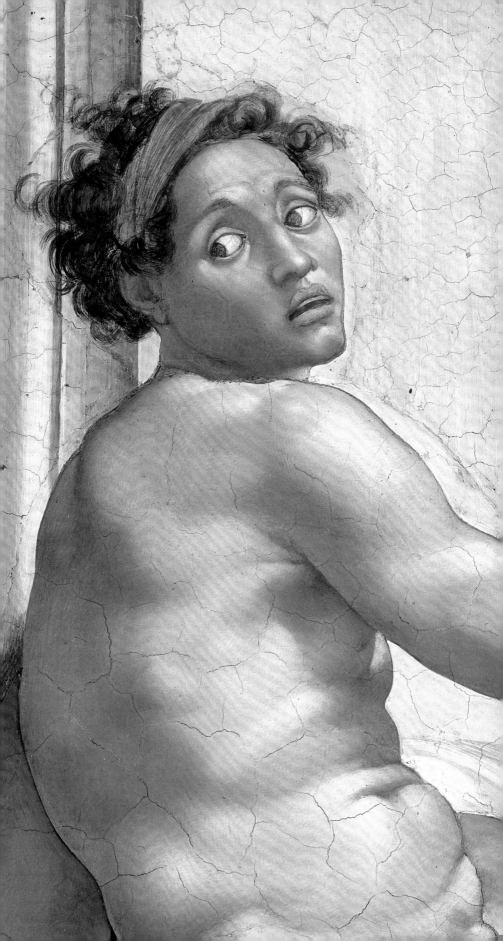

Ignudi above the Prophet Ezekiel

Ignudi above the Cumaean Sibyl

Ignudi above the Persian Sibyl

Ignudi above the Prophet Daniel

Zachariah

Zachariah 9, 9:
Rejoice greatly, O daughter of Sion, shout for joy, O daughter of Jerusalem: behold thy King will come to thee, the just and saviour. He is poor, riding upon an ass, and upon a colt, the foal of an ass.

The Delphic Sibyl

Joel

Joel 2, 19:
And the Lord answered and said to his people: "Behold, I will send you corn, and wine, and oil, and you shall be filled with them; and I will no longer make you a reproach among the nations".

Isaiah

Isaiah 53, 5:
But he was wounded for our iniquities, he was bruised for our sins. The chastisement of our peace was upon him, and by his bruises we are healed.

Eritrean Sibyl

… and keeping a book at a distance, she tries to turn a page, while with crossed knees she is seriously pondering about what to write until a child behind her blowing over a fire brand lights up the lamp.
(Giorgio Vasari, *Vita di Michelangelo Buonarroti fiorentino*, 1568, publisher Bettarini - Barocchi 1987, p. 44)

Cumaean Sibyl

… she is an old and very beautiful sibyl, who, while she is sitting down, studies the book with excessive grace and with two children in a beautiful pose who are around her.

(Giorgio Vasari, *Vita di Michelangelo Buonarroti fiorentino*, 1568, publisher Bettarini - Barocchi, 1987, p. 45)

Ezekiel

Ezekiel 40, 4:

And this man said to me: "Son of man see with thy eyes and hear with thy ears, and set thy heart upon all that I shall show thee; for thou art brought hither that they may be shown to thee; declare all that thou seest to the house of Israel".

Daniel

Daniel 10, 21; 11, 1:
But I will tell thee what is set down in the scripture of truth; and none is my helper in all these things but Michael your prince. And from the first year of Darius Mede I stood up that he might be strengthened and confirmed.

Persian Sibyl

... where wanting to express age, in addition to wrapping her in robes, he wanted to show how her blood was frozen by time, and in addition in reading, for having seen her already weary, he carefully made her put the book close to her eyes. (Giorgio Vasari, *Vita di Michelangelo Buonarroti fiorentino*, 1568, publisher Bettarini - Barocchi, 1987, p. 43)

Libyan Sibyl

... who, having written a great number taken from many books posing in a feminine way, standing up and at the same time showing she wants to get up and grab the book - something that is very difficult, if not impossible, for anybody else except her master. (Giorgio Vasari, *Vita di Michelangelo Buonrarroti fiorentino*, 1568, publisher Bettarini - Barocchi 1987, p. 45, p. 46)

LIBICA

Jeremiah

Jeremiah 20, 14-15:
Cursed be the day wherein I was born; let the day in which my mother bore me be blessed.
Cursed be the man who brought the tidings to my father saying "A man child is born to thee" and made him greatly rejoice.

Jonah

Jonah 3, 5; 10:
And the men of Ninive believed in God and they proclaimed a fast and put on sackcloth from the greatest to the least … And God saw their works that they were turned from their evil way; and God had mercy with regard to the evil which he had said he would do to them, and he did it not.

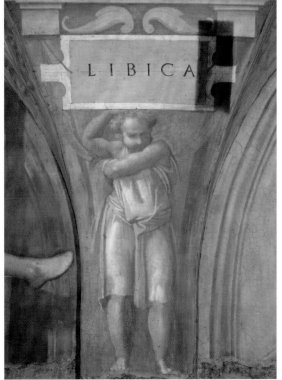

Putti

*Spandrel above the Lunette
of Jesse, David and Solomon*

*Spandrel above the Lunette
of Josiah, Jechoniah and Shealtiel*

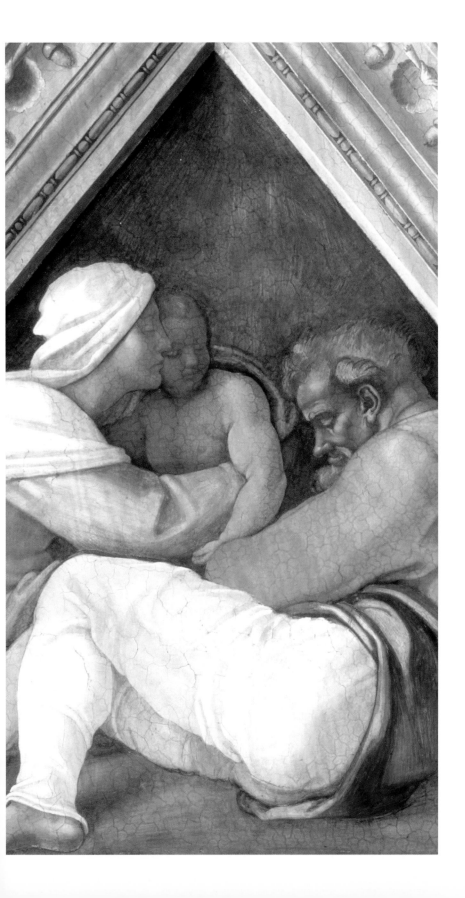

*Lunette of Jesse, David
and Solomon*

Lunette of Hezekiah,
Manasseh and Amon

Lunette of Azor and Zadok

The *Last Judgement*

In 1533 Michelangelo was summoned by Pope Clement VII (de' Medici 1523-1534) to paint the Sistine Chapel anew, although this time he would be working on the far wall, behind the altar.

The first indication that the Pope intended to assign the work to the master can be gleaned in a letter that the painter and Michelangelo's friend Sebastiano del Piombo (Sebastiano Luciani, known as del Piombo, 1485-1547) wrote to the Tuscan artist on 17 July 1533, informing the latter of the pontiff's intention to "contract you to such a thing that you could never ever dream about".

The task was probably mapped out during the meeting between Michelangelo and Clement VII that took place in San Miniato al Tedesco towards the end of September 1533; consisting in the realisation of the *Last Judgement* on the altar wall of the Chapel. The project must have already been at an advanced stage in February 1534, given that Nino Sernini, agent of the Gonzaga family at the pontifical court, reported that Buonarroti had accepted the task of painting 'a resurrection', by which he meant not that of Christ, but the resurrection of the flesh on the day of the Last Judgement. Furthermore, it is Sernini who informs us of the setting up at that time of the scaffolding necessary for the realisation of the fresco. Condivi recalls that Clement VII, prior to passing away in September 1534, had already examined a design by Michelangelo; in all probability a model. In a successive planning phase, as documented by a sketch of the fresco dated 1534 and conserved in Casa Buonarroti (Florence), Michelangelo describes the altar wall of the Chapel. The composition consists of a semi-circular form around the figure of Christ, and does not yet envisage the occupation of the space of the two lunettes, frescoed by Buonarroti himself together with the vault about twenty years earlier; while the framed opening at the centre of the lower section of the design makes reference to the altar-piece showing the *Assumption of the Virgin Mary* painted by Perugino at the time of Sixtus IV. In this early phase of the work, Michelangelo thus intended to save these two pre-existing pictorial episodes, which would have been integrated with the new intervention. However, the subsequent definitive model sacrificed the entire preceding decoration and, as soon as this was approved by the Pope, saw Michelangelo move to Rome, in September 1534, to begin work, thereby leaving interrupted in Florence, as Vasari recounts, his work on the New Sacristy and Laurentian Library.

Just two days after his arrival, however, Clement VII died, and on hearing this Michelangelo considered himself free to dedicate himself to the completion of perhaps his most tragic work, the Tomb of Julius II. The new pontiff Paul III (Farnese, 1534-1549) insisted that the projected *Last Judgement* should not be abandoned. In any case Michelangelo only commenced work in the Chapel in November 1536, eliminating the XV Century pictorial interventions that covered the walls. In order to prepare for the new work, the two windows were filled in, while the two lunettes which had been painted together with the vault were removed. The master accepted – not without some initial resistance – this serious assignment, given that he was by now nearly sixty, and in a moment when great incomplete projects were beginning to weigh upon him. Added to these preoccupations was his proverbial reluctance when faced with painting, and for this reason he requested the collaboration of his friend Sebastiano del Piombo. It is not clear what the exact role of the Venetian painter was. Given that he was a mature and recognised artist, it is possible to hypothesise that he undertook duties analogous to those carried out by Granacci during the painting of the vault. Vasari recounts that Sebastiano oversaw the work for the preparation of the wall's surface, making it ready to be painted with oil, using the Nordic technique which he himself had experimented. This provoked great resentment on the part of Michelangelo, who wanted to paint use the fresco technique and asserted that "colouring using oil was the art of women and of well-to-do and slothful people, such as Brother Bastiano". This disagreement of a technical nature (but which also implied opposing modes of conceiving the art of painting) led to the definitive rupture of a twenty-year friendship between the two artists, and to the Tuscan master once more labouring alone. Michelangelo created an autonomous space, independent of the physical limits imposed by the Chapel, conceived as a grandiose vision in which the second coming of Christ at the end of time is depicted. He renounces the architectonic scansion customary in the rest of the frescoed surface, and instead turns to a blue lapis lazzuli background, against which he organises the composition around large blocks of figures; in total Michelangelo painted over two hundred. To every block corresponds a precise stage in the process of salvation and damnation. The overall effect is anything but static; the fluid movement of souls from one zone to another creates a linking continuity between the various groups.

If identification of Michelangelo's literary sources appears complex – *in primis* the *Divine Comedy* – it is highly likely that the artist had looked at previous representations of the *Last Judgement*, in which a composition consisting of superimposed zones was very rigorous, with a clear separation of the zone of the Elect from that of the Damned. Such an iconography was to be completely revolutionised, thanks to an absolutely dynamic approach. Starting from the top, in the two lunettes, several angels without wings sustain the symbols of the Passion of Christ and of the Redemption of humanity; the cross, the whipping-post, and the crown of thorns. Underneath them, around the fulcrum made up of Christ the Judge and Our Lady of the Assumption, the celestial court unfolds, crowded with saints, martyrs and the blessed. At the centre, the pivot of the composition is Christ. Ideally seated on a throne of clouds, He turns His head and left hand towards the group of saints placed at his side, while His right hand is raised in an imperious gesture, leading to a decisive rotating of the figure's bust, from which is generated the sense of movement of the entire scene. Here Michelangelo depicts the decisive moment in human experience as a swirling vortex, which departs from the gesture of the Omnipotent, and involves the whole of humanity in a motion which is both rising and falling at the same time.

Recognisable on the left is John the Baptist with his fur cloak. In the centre is St. Laurence with the gridiron of his martyrdom, and

The Last Judgement

alongside St. Bartholomew, holding the skin that was stripped from him while still alive, the head of which is thought to be a self-portrait of Buonarroti. To the right is St. Peter with the keys, while below St. Catherine of Alessandria is depicted with the toothed wheel. At her shoulders stands St. Biagio. Descending can be seen several angels, sounding the trumpets of judgement. Their faces deformed by the effort, they arouse the dead, while two archangels bear the book with the names of the Elect, and a second, somewhat more voluminous, listing the Damned. To the left are the Elect rising to heaven, to the right the Damned are shoved by the angels towards a hell in which can be discerned Dantesque citations. The most notable is the image of the diabolical ferryman of the nether world Charon, who pushes the Damned into the presence of Minos, the infernal judge who, according to Vasari, has the features

Angels with Symbols
of the Passion

of the Pope's chamberlain Biagio da Cesena, culpable of criticising Michelangelo's work. Notable is the difference in height between the figures in this part – a little over a metre-and-a-half – and those in the register above, which were up to a metre taller, so as to be easily seen from the ground.

The standard iconography of the Last Judgement of the XIV and XV Centuries would appear to have been superseded by the whirling rhythm impressed by Christ's peremptory gesture. With the exception of the resurrection of the flesh on the lower left, and the infernal scene on the opposite side, all the figures float without halting, in unusual and foreshortened poses, against the abstract background of a brilliant sky in lapis lazuli; in breathless upward motion or in the obstinate struggle against the angels, so as to avoid falling into an infernal nether region. In the absence of a landscape clearly defined in perspective, or of an identifiable light source, it is the human body that provides the 'yardstick' of the composition; the naked body, which conjoined with the soul, is rendered perfect and 'ideal', regardless of differences in age or sex. It was perhaps too risky an interpretation for the intransigent dignitaries of the

papal court, who were about to meet in council to reaffirm the
orthodoxy of the church in the face of attacks from Lutherans. They
were quick to criticise Michelangelo's masterpiece for its exclusive
concentration upon the preoccupations and difficulties of art itself,
and for its failure to make any attempt to solicit devotion.
On the 31 October 1541, the finished fresco was presented
to the Pope, who organised the celebration of Vespers in the
renovated Chapel. Its fame was instantly widespread. Before it was
officially unveiled, the *Last Judgement* had already aroused fierce
criticism of a moral nature. The nudity of the personages, which
in Michelangelo's view possessed a spiritual value, was considered
scandalous, and not consonant with the subject, the setting or, in
general, the times. In those years, in fact, the Church was engaged
in the battle with Lutheran Doctrine, and also had to defend
itself against accusations of corruption and immorality. Many
felt that the *Last Judgement* did not respond to these exigencies.
Michelangelo did not take easily to this criticism, and decided to
get his own back on the previously cited papal chamberlain, Biagio
da Cesena. Nevertheless, the contemporary cultural community
welcomed the work as a new masterpiece, so much so that the great
Venetian master Titian (Tiziano Vecellio, c.1480-1576), according
to an anecdote, in front of the *Judgement* exclaimed: "Oh iniquitous
destiny, if time must corrupt and destroy even this!". As Vasari
recounts in his biography of Buonarroti, from the middle of the
1500s, painters who came to Rome never failed to go in pilgrimage
to the Vatican in order to admire at first hand the imposing fresco.
The polemic ignited by the accusations of licentiousness may
have angered its author, but at the same time could not help but
increase the fame of the work, which became heavily requested on
the artistic market; being reproduced in prints, in miniature and
in painting. However, on 21 January 1564, a few weeks before the
death of Michelangelo on 18 February, the congregation of the
Council of Trent (1545-1563) decided to cover those parts of the
fresco which were deemed obscene. The task of covering up such
nudity with a sort of breeches (maintained in the final restoration
from 1990 to 1994) was given to Daniele da Volterra, for which
he earned the unflattering nickname 'Braghettone' (the breeches-
maker). Yet Daniele was a much-loved friend of Michelangelo, the
last and most faithful, who assisted him at his death. The increase
in the accusations of 'inconvenience' had led the inquisitorial court
to purge such infamy, making use of the hand of the painter closest
to the master, and thus considered most suitable to approach the
modifications envisaged with maximum respect and competence.
Just a few months later, in April 1566, the artist from Volterra also
died, leaving among his property, conserved like a holy relic, a
fragment of the knee sculpted by his older and more authoritative
friend for the Christ of the Vatican Pietà, which was subsequently
abandoned.
On 8 April 1994 John Paul II inaugurated with a solemn mass the
Sistine Chapel at the conclusion of the most admired, but at the
same time most contested restoration of the XX Century, the final
result of which – as writes Antonio Paolucci, Director of the Vatican
Museums – "can be considered one of the greatest and happiest
enterprises of the 1900s".

Christ as Judge

Mark 13, 24-27:
But in those days, after that time of distress, the
sun will be darkened, the moon will not give its
light, the stars will come falling out of the sky
and the powers in the heavens will be shaken.
And then he will send the angels to gather his
elect from the four winds.

The Blessed on the Right

Wisdom 5, 16:
So they will receive the glorious crown and the
diadem of beauty from the Lord's hand; and he
will shelter them with his right hand and with his
arm he will shield them.

The Joy of the Saved

1 Letter of Peter 4, 13:
Be glad, so that you may enjoy a much greater
gladness when his glory is revealed.

The Saved who ascend to Heaven

1 Thessalonians 4, 16-17:
Those who have died in Christ will be the first to
rise, and only after that shall we who remain alive
be taken up in the clouds, together with them, to
meet the Lord in the air.
This is the way we shall be with the Lord for ever.

The Condemned who descend into Hell

Matthew 13, 41-42:
The Son of man will send his angels and they
will gather out of his kingdom all causes of falling
and all who do evil, and throw them into the
blazing furnace, where there will be weeping and
gnashing of teeth.

Angels with Trumpets

Matthew 24, 31:
And he will send his angels with a loud trumpet
to gather his elect from the four winds, from one
end of heaven to the other.

Resurrection of Bodies

Ezekiel 37, 7-8; 12:
I prophesied as I had been ordered. While I was
prophesying there was a noise, a clattering sound;
it was the bones coming together.
And as I looked, they were covered with sinews;
flesh was growing on them and skin was covering
them … "said the Lord: And you will know that
I am Yahweh, when I have opened your graves
and caused you to come up out of your graves"…

Demons' Den

Matthew 8, 11-12:
And I tell you that many will come from east and
west and sit down … in the kingdom of heaven;
but the children of the kingdom will be thrown
out into the darkness outside, where there will be
weeping and gnashing of teeth.

Hell

Matthew 13, 50:
… to throw them into the blazing
furnace, where there will be weeping and
gnashing of teeth.